Collins

easy learning

Maths

Ages 8–10

1.5 kg = 1500 g

Sarah-Anne Fernandes

How to use this book

This book is for parents who want to work with their child at home to support and practise what is happening at school.

- Ask your child what maths they are doing at school and choose an appropriate topic. Tackle one topic at a time.

- Help with reading the instructions where necessary, and ensure that your child understands what to do.

- Help and encourage your child to check their own answers as they complete each activity. Discuss with your child what they have learnt.

- Let your child return to their favourite pages once they have been completed, to play the games and talk about the activities.

- Reward your child with plenty of praise and encouragement.

Special features

- **Games:** There is a game on each double page that reinforces the maths topic. Each game is for two players, unless otherwise indicated. Some of the games require a spinner, which is easily made using the circles printed on the games pages, a pencil and a paper clip. Gently flick the paper clip with your finger to make it spin.

- At the bottom of every page you will find footnotes that are **Parent's notes**. These are divided into '**What you need to know**', which explain the key maths idea, and '**Taking it further**', which suggest activities and encourage discussion with your child about what they have learnt. The words in bold are key words that you should focus on when talking to your child.

ACKNOWLEDGEMENTS

The author and publisher are grateful to the copyright holders for permission to use quoted materials and images.

p.7 © Shutterstock.com/sean biggs; p.8 © Credit required. Clipart.com; p.8 © owatta/Shutterstock.com; p.10 © Atid28/Shutterstock.com; p.11 © Zern Liew/Shutterstock.com; p.16 © Shutterstock.com/HitToon.com; p.17 © Alexzel/Shutterstock.com; p.19 © Lori Mittan Studio/Shutterstock.com; p.22 © Zern Liew/Shutterstock.com; p.22 © Shutterstock.com/Art'nLera; p.27 © owatta/Shutterstock.com; p.27 © 2009 Jupiterimages Corporation; p.28 © iralu/Shutterstock.com; p.33 © 2008 Jupiterimages Corporation; p.36 © Anton Brand/Shutterstock.com; p.36 © wanpatsorn/Shutterstock

Every effort has been made to trace copyright holders and obtain their permission for the use of copyright material. The author and publisher will gladly receive information enabling them to rectify any error or omission in subsequent editions. All facts are correct at time of going to press.

Published by Collins
An imprint of HarperCollinsPublishers
1 London Bridge Street
London SE1 9GF

© HarperCollinsPublishers Limited 2014

ISBN 9780007559824

First published 2014

10 9 8 7 6 5

British Library Cataloguing in Publication Data.

A CIP record of this book is available from the British Library.

Publishing manager: Rebecca Skinner
Author: Sarah-Anne Fernandes (SolveMaths Ltd)
Assistant author: Gareth Fernandes (SolveMaths Ltd)
Commissioning and series editor: Charlotte Christensen
Project editor and manager: David Mantovani
Cover design: Susi Martin and Paul Oates
Inside concept design: Lodestone Publishing Limited and Paul Oates
Text design and layout: Q2A Media Services Pvt. Ltd.
Artwork: Rachel Annie Bridgen, Q2A Media Services
Production: Karen Nulty
Printed in Great Britain by Martins the Printers

MIX
Paper from responsible source
FSC® C007454

This book is produced from independently certified FSC™ paper to ensure responsible forest management.

For more information visit:
www.harpercollins.co.uk/green

Contents

Numbers beyond 1000	4
Adding and subtracting 1000	6
Rounding whole numbers	8
Number patterns	10
Decimals	12
Addition and subtraction	14
Multiplication and division facts	16
Multiplying and dividing by 10 and 100	18
Multiplying and dividing larger numbers	20
Problem solving	22
Fractions	24
More fractions	26
Area and perimeter	28
Measures	30
Money	32
Time	34
More problem solving	36
Angles	38
Quadrilaterals and triangles	40
Symmetry	42
Coordinates	44
Graphs	46
Answers	48

Numbers beyond 1000

Place value

- Write the value of the digit 3 in each of these numbers.

1346	5432	2793	3782
300	30	3	3000

- Write the value of the digit 9 in each of these numbers.

9081	7923	8179	1695
9000	900	9	90

Comparing and ordering

- Put these numbers and measures into the correct order.

Boxes labelled: 1112, 1172, 1010, 1023

Most			Least
1172	1112	1023	1010

Signposts labelled: 8541 m, 9754 m, 9876 m, 8692 m

Longest			Shortest
9876	9754	8692	8541

Trucks labelled: 6010 kg, 7257 kg, 5334 kg, 7957 kg

Heaviest			Lightest
7957 kg	7257 kg	6010 kg	5334k

Game: Crooked rules!

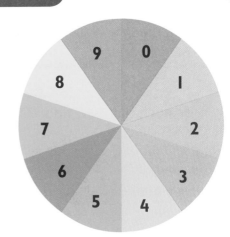

You need: a paper clip, a pencil, paper.

- Make a copy of the playing board below.
- Take turns to spin the spinner.
- Write the digit spun on your playing board. Choose the best place to write your digit – you can write it on your row or your opponent's row.
- When the playing board is full, the player with the larger number wins.

> **TIP**: Think about your tactics in this game. For example, if you roll '1', will you keep this or will you put it in one of your opponent's place value columns? Remember, the aim is to make the largest number!

	Thousands	Hundreds	Tens	Ones
Player 1				
Player 2				

Missing numbers

Jolly joke

Which snakes are the best at doing sums?

Adders!

- Fill in the missing numbers.

3753 = $\boxed{3000}$ + 700 + 50 + 3

5967 = 5000 + $\boxed{400}$ + 60 + 7

4639 = 4000 + 600 + $\boxed{30}$ + 9

1398 = 1000 + 300 + 90 + $\boxed{8}$

Taking it further Use the 'Crooked rules!' board again. Play with an opponent. Spin the spinner four times to make a 4-digit number, then let your opponent do the same. Look at the numbers that have been made and decide whether to use **less than** (<), **more than** (>) or **equal to** (=) between the two scores. For example, player 1 spins the digits 1, 3, 2 and 6 to make the number 1326. Player 2 spins the digits 5, 2, 4 and 1 to make the number 5241. Therefore, 1326 < 5241.

5

Adding and subtracting 1000

For each number, find 1000 more.

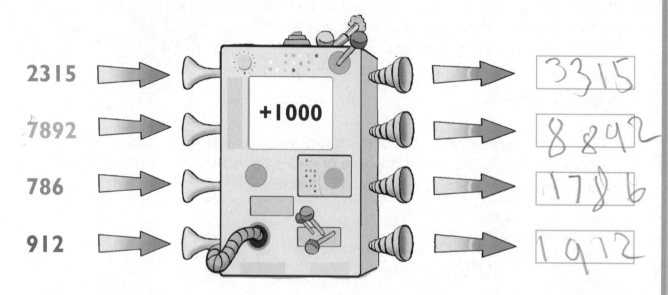

	+1000	
2315	→	3315
7892	→	8892
786	→	1786
912	→	1912

1000 less

For each number, find 1000 less.

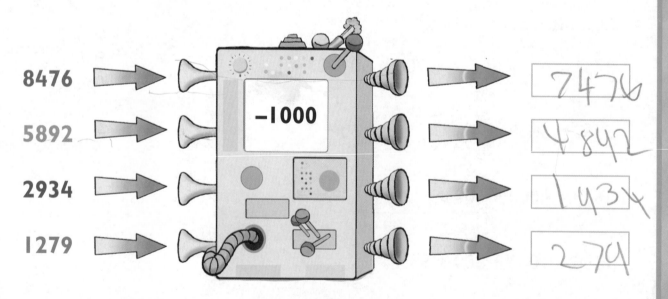

	−1000	
8476	→	7476
5892	→	4892
2934	→	1434
1279	→	279

What you need to know   At this stage your child is learning to find **1000 more** or **1000 less** than a given number. This will help your child with adding and subtracting larger numbers and estimating whether their answers are correct.

Game: Bank accounts

You need: a 1–6 dice, a paper clip, a pencil, paper, a different coloured counter each.

- Take turns to roll the dice and move your counter the number of spaces rolled from the 'start' position.

- Spin the spinner and work out either £1000 more or £1000 less than the amount of money you landed on. Write this on your piece of paper.

- After three goes each, add up the total money saved in your bank account. The player with more money wins!

£1000 less	£1000 more
£1000 more	£1000 less

START →	£2567	£4136	£3098	£6274	£1463	£4191
£2153						£7285
£3829						£5929
£9143	£8901	£6666	£7243	£5916	£1421	£9806	£4136

Jolly joke

What travels around the world but stays in a corner?

A stamp!

True or false

- Put a tick ✓ by the statements that are **true** and a cross ✗ by the statements that are **false**.

1000 more than 4000 is the same as 1000 less than 6000.

1000 less than 3560 is the same as 1000 more than 1560.

1000 less than 4192 is the same as 1000 more than 1192. ✗

Taking it further Look again at the true and false statements. Ask your child to correct the statement that is false. Ask them to make up their own 'True or false' statement game about + 1000 / – 1000 that they can play with their friends.

Rounding whole numbers

Rounding 3-digit numbers to the nearest 10 and 100

- Round each distance to the nearest 10 km and 100 km.

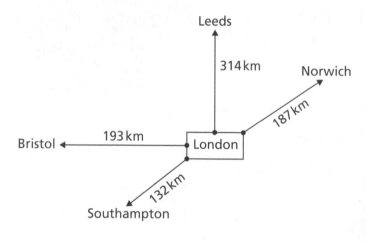

	10 km	100 km
London to Norwich	190	200 km
London to Bristol	190 km	200 km
London to Leeds	310 km	300 km
London to Southampton	130 km	100 k

Rounding 4-digit numbers to the nearest 10, 100 and 1000

- Round each sum of money to the nearest £10, £100 and £1000.

£1672

£5238

	£10	£100	£1000
TV	£1670	£1700	£2000
Motorbike	£5240	£5200	£5000

What you need to know   At this stage your child is learning to round any number to the nearest 10, 100 or 1000. Encourage your child to remember to **round down** when the place value column is less than 5 and **round up** when it is 5 or more.

- When rounding to the nearest 10, look at the place value of the ones column. For example, 142 rounded to the nearest 10 is 140 because 2 ones (units) is less than 5 ones (units); it is closer to 140 than 150 on a number line.
- When rounding to the nearest 100, look at the place value of the tens column. For example, 142 rounded to the nearest 100 is 100 because 4 tens is less than 5 tens.
- When rounding to the nearest 1000 look at the place value of the hundreds column. For example, 3826 rounded to the nearest 1000 is 4000 because 8 hundreds is more than 5 hundreds.

Game: Planets and stars

You need: a paper clip, a 1–6 dice, five different coloured counters each, a pencil, paper.

- Take turns to spin the spinner four times: the first number spun is the units, the second number is the tens, the third is the hundreds and the fourth is the thousands. Write down your number.

- Round the number to the nearest 1000 or 100 and place a counter over a matching planet or star. If a planet or star is already covered up, miss a turn.

- The first player to cover one planet and four stars wins!

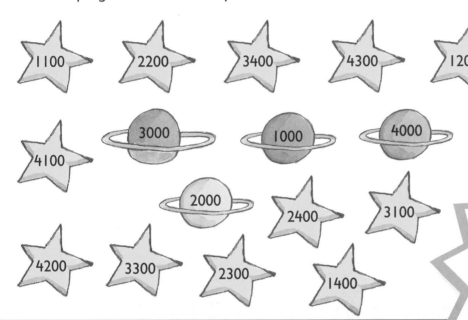

Jolly joke

How do 17 sheep become 20 sheep?

When you round them up!

Rounding possibilities

- List ten numbers that give 980 when rounded to the nearest 10.

985 986 987 988 989 981
982 983 986 980

- List ten numbers that give 700 when rounded to the nearest 10.

695 696 697 698 699 700
700 702 703 704

Taking it further Ask your child to list as many numbers as possible that give 2000 when rounded to the nearest 1000. Encourage your child to be systematic. Can they think of an efficient way of writing the possible numbers using the symbols **less than (<)**, **more than (>)** and **equal to (=)**?

Number patterns

- Fill in the missing numbers in these sequences.

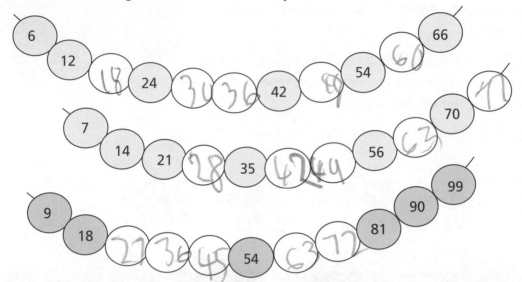

6, 12, 18, 24, 30, 36, 42, 48, 54, 60, 66

7, 14, 21, 28, 35, 42, 49, 56, 63, 70, 77

9, 18, 27, 36, 45, 54, 63, 72, 81, 90, 99

Negative numbers

- Continue the number sequences.

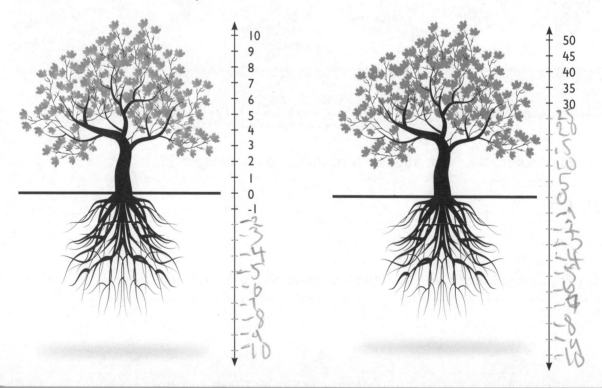

10 9 8 7 6 5 4 3 2 1 0 -1 -2 -3 -4 -5 -6 -7 -8 -9 -10

50 45 40 35 30 25 20 15 10 5 0 -5 -10 -15 -20 -25

What you need to know At this stage your child is learning to count in **multiples of 6**, **7**, **9**, **25** and **1000**. It is important to encourage your child to count on from **different multiple starting points** so that they are not always starting at zero. Your child is also learning to count below zero and use negative neumbers (e.g. in the context of temperature).

Game: Scrunch

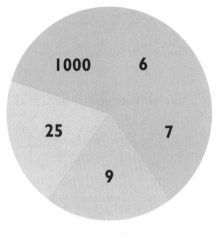

You need: a paper clip, a pencil, paper.

- Scrunch up a piece of paper to make a ball.

- Player 1 spins the spinner to find the multiple you will be counting in.

- Player 1 starts at '0' and then throws the paper ball to player 2, who says the next multiple in the sequence. Stop at the 12th multiple in each sequence. For example, if you are counting in multiples of 6 you will stop at 72.

- Player 2 now spins the spinner to find the next multiple.

- Both players continue to play until all the multiples on the spinner have been counted.

Jolly joke

What did seven, eight and nine say to thirty?

You are really out of order!

Dice magic

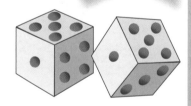

Follow the instructions below.

> Roll two dice. Write down the two numbers on the **tops** of the dice and the two numbers on the **bottoms** of the dice. Add these four numbers together.
>
> Repeat several times.

- What pattern do you notice with all the totals?
Can you explain why this pattern is forming?

_____

_____

_____

Taking it further Find as many dice as possible – up to five would be good. Using what they learnt from the 'Dice magic' activity, ask your child what they think will be the total of the numbers on the **tops** and the **bottoms** of the dice if they roll three dice? What about if they roll four or five dice? Ask your child to check if their guesses are correct by rolling the appropriate number of dice and then adding up the numbers from the tops and bottoms. What number do they need to multiply by each time?

Decimals

Place value

- Write the value of the digit 7 in each of these decimal numbers.

0.72	8.67	7.54	17.24	0.07
0.7	0.07	7	7	0.07

Comparing and ordering

- Put these numbers and measures into the correct order.

3.12 kg   3.22 kg   3.70 kg   2.86 kg

Heaviest 3.70 KG   3.22 KG 3.12 Kg 2.86 Kg Lightest

£2.56   £2.01   £2.81   £2.79

Most £2.81 £2.79 £2.56 £2.01 Least

4.84ℓ   3.25ℓ   4.95ℓ   4.85ℓ

Most 4.95 4.85 4.84 3.25 Least

What you need to know   At this stage your child is learning to recognise and use **decimals**. They are learning the value of digits in a number with up to **two decimal places**. For example, 21.76 = 20 (2 tens), 1 (one unit), 0.7 (7 **tenths**) and 0.06 (6 **hundredths**). They will use this knowledge to help them order and compare numbers.

Game: Rounding wheel!

You need: a paper clip, eight different coloured counters each, a pencil.

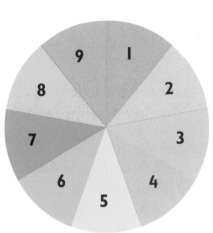

- Take turns to spin the spinner twice and make a decimal number.

- Round your decimal number to the nearest whole number.

- Place a counter on the matching number on the Ferris wheel. If the number on the wheel is already covered, miss a turn.

- The player who covers more numbers on the Ferris wheel wins!

Example: If you spin 7 and 6 you can make either 6.7 or 7.6 as your decimal number. 6.7 rounded to the nearest whole number is 7; 7.6 rounded to the nearest whole number is 8.

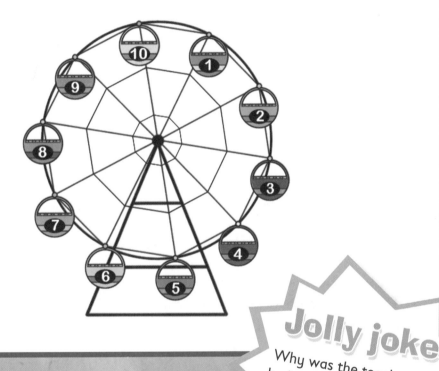

Jolly joke

Why was the teacher so bad at teaching decimals?

He couldn't get the point across.

Within limits

- Write seven different decimal numbers that are greater than 5 but less than 5.5. An example has been done for you.

5.21	5.25
5.22	5.26
5.23	5.27
5.24	5.29

5
5.5

Taking it further Look at a shopping receipt with your child and order the prices on the receipt from most expensive to cheapest. Ask them what coins represent the tenths and hundredths columns.

Addition and subtraction

Adding large whole numbers

- Answer the following using column addition.
The first one has been done for you.

$257 + 152 =$ 409

```
    1
  2 5 7
+ 1 5 2
  4 0 9
```

$4354 + 452 =$ 4806

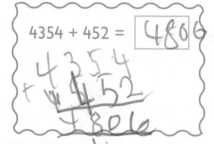

$5715 + 1284 =$ 6999

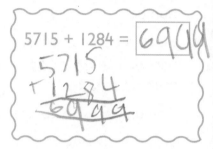

$1249 + 2539 =$ 3788

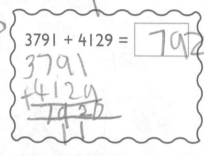

$3791 + 4129 =$ 7920

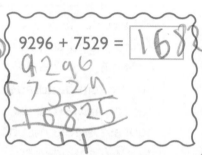

$9296 + 7529 =$ 16825

Subtracting large whole numbers

- Answer the following using column subtraction.
The first one has been done for you.

$2838 - 1294 =$ 1544

```
    7 1
  2 8 3 8
- 1 2 9 4
  1 5 4 4
```

$4239 - 178 =$ 4061

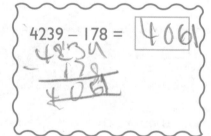

$5678 - 3465 =$ 2213

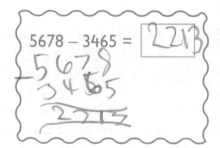

$7984 - 6879 =$ 1105

$2591 - 1885 =$ 706

$7862 - 3991 =$ 3871

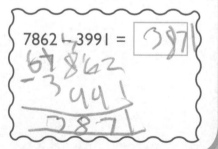

Game: Pop concert tickets

You need: two paper clips, two pencils, paper.

The best pop bands are playing in a concert on Saturday. There are 2437 tickets available. *Radio None* and *Blues FM* are giving away tickets all week to competition winners.

- Take turns to spin both of the stations' spinners and find the total number of tickets the two radio stations have given away. Calculate how many tickets are left to sell.

- The player who has more tickets left to sell wins a point.

- Play five rounds. The player who has more points wins!

Radio None

931	378
589	784

Blues FM

1024	906
599	672

Jolly joke

Why is 2 + 2 = 5 like your left foot?

It's not right!

Missing digits

- Use the inverse process to find the missing digits in each calculation.

```
  4 ★ 6 7
-   6 8 4
  4 0 8 3
```

★ = 6

```
  9 ★ 3 ★
+ 4 5 8 7
 13 8 2 5
```

★ = 2

★ = 8

```
  8  7  4  1
+ 1 ★  ★  1
 10  2  3  2
```

★ = 4

★ = 9

Taking it further Ask your child real-life word problems involving one step or two steps (see page 22). Try to use a range of vocabulary for addition (e.g. total, sum, altogether, more than) and subtraction (e.g. less than, take away, difference between).

Multiplication and division facts

Multiplication grid

- Complete this multiplication grid.

×	1	2	3	4	5	6	7	8	9	10	11	12
2	2		6	8		12	14		18		22	24
3	3	6		12		18	21	24		30	33	
4	4		12	16	20	24		32	36		44	48
5		10	15			30	35			50		60
6	6		18	24	30		42	48	54	60		72
7	7		21	28	35	42		56		70	77	
8		16			40	48			72			96
9	9	18	27	36	45		63	72	81	90		
10	10		30	40		60	70		90	100	110	120
11	11	22		44	55		77	88		110		
12		24	36				84					

Division detective

- Use the multiplication grid above to find 15 different division facts.

  Remember: if you know 6 × 4 = 24 then you know the division fact 24 ÷ 4 = 6

What you need to know At this stage your child is learning to recall **multiplication** and **division facts** for all the multiplications up to **12 × 12**. However, remember your child will have already learnt the 2, 3, 4, 5, 8 and 10 multiplication tables, so these tables are being revised. The multiplication tables that will be new at this stage are **6, 7, 9, 11** and **12**. Your child is also learning to recognise **factor pairs**. For example, the factor pairs of 16 are 1 × 16, 2 × 8 and 4 × 4.

16

Game: Moving across the road

You need: a paper clip, a pencil.

- Player 1 spins the spinner and circles the number on their playing board that matches the number on the spinner.

- Spin the spinner again. This time multiply the number circled on your playing board by the number shown on the spinner.

- Say out loud the answer. If your partner agrees with your answer then cross out the number that is circled and write the answer in the opposite box across the road.

- Player 2 now has their turn.

- Keep taking turns. If you spin a number that has already been moved across the road then miss a go.

- The first player to move all their numbers across the road wins!

Player 1

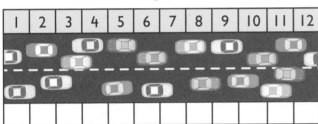

1	2	3	4	5	6	7	8	9	10	11	12

Player 2

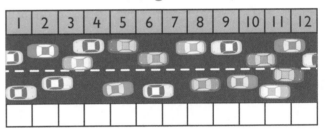

1	2	3	4	5	6	7	8	9	10	11	12

Herb pot factor pairs

Jolly joke

Why should you wear glasses for maths?

They improve di-vision!

- Complete the missing factor pairs for each herb pot.

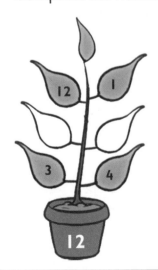

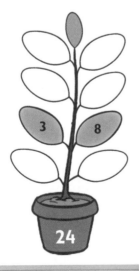

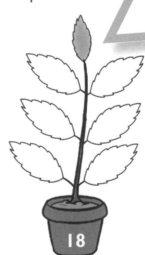

Taking it further Play 'Moving across the road' again, practising the multiplication tables that your child is not fully confident with yet. Also ask your child to round each 'product' (the answer to each multiplication table fact) to the nearest 10.

Multiplying and dividing by 10 and 100

Multiplying by 10 and 100

- Multiply each number by 10 or 100.

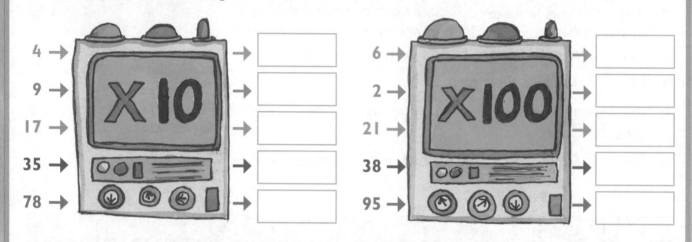

4 →   →
9 →   →
17 →   →
35 →   →
78 →   →

6 →   →
2 →   →
21 →   →
38 →   →
95 →   →

Dividing by 10 and 100

- Divide each number by 10 or 100.

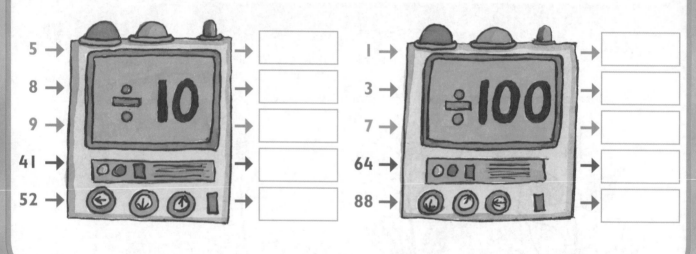

5 →   →
8 →   →
9 →   →
41 →   →
52 →   →

1 →   →
3 →   →
7 →   →
64 →   →
88 →   →

What you need to know At this stage your child is learning to understand the effects of **multiplying** and **dividing** a 1-digit number or 2-digit number by 10 and 100. Encourage your child to move the digits to the left when multiplying and to the right when dividing. Remind your child to put in the 0 as a **place value holder**. For example, the diagram shows the effects of multiplying and dividing 5 by 10 and 100.

1000	100	10	1	0.1	0.01
			5 •		
		5	0 •			5 × 10
	5	0	0 •			5 × 100
			0 •	5		5 ÷ 10
			0 •	0	5	5 ÷ 100

Game: Race to the moon

You need: a paper clip, a pencil, four counters each.

- Each player should choose a rocket colour (red or green).
- Take turns to spin a number. Multiply or divide the number on the start rocket by the number spun.
- Put a counter on the rocket with the correct answer. If your answer rocket is already covered, then miss a go.
- Keep taking turns, each time multiplying or dividing the number on the start rocket.
- The winner is the first player to have counters on all their rockets (excluding the start rocket).

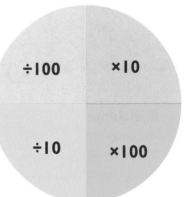

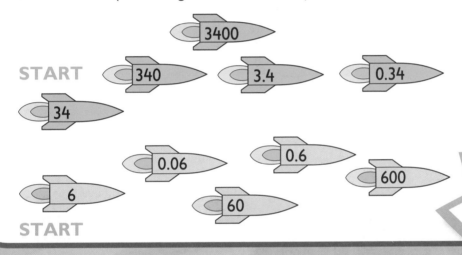

Jolly joke
Why are you doing multiplication on the floor?

You told me not to use tables!

Toy boxes

A carpenter is making two toy boxes. She has some measurements in metres and some in centimetres.

- Convert the measurements so she has the same units for each box.

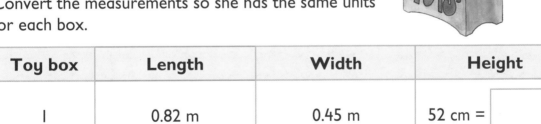

Toy box	Length	Width	Height
1	0.82 m	0.45 m	52 cm = ⬚ m
2	0.76 m = ⬚ cm	52 cm	61 cm

Taking it further   Ask your child how many pence are in one pound and then get them to use their knowledge of ×100 and ÷100 to convert pounds to pence and pence to pounds. For example, £4 = 400p (4 × 100p), £46 = 4600p (46 × 100p); 500p = £5 (500p ÷ 100); 7200p = £72 (7200p ÷ 100).

Multiplying and dividing larger numbers

Multiplying larger numbers

- Calculate these multiplications. The first one has been done for you.

316 × 4 = $\boxed{1264}$

$$\begin{array}{r} {\scriptstyle 2} \\ 3\ 1\ 6 \\ \times \quad 4 \\ \hline 1\ 2\ 6\ 4 \end{array}$$

68 × 7 = ☐

314 × 6 = ☐

527 × 7 = ☐

185 × 8 = ☐

279 × 9 = ☐

Dividing larger numbers

- Calculate these divisions. The first one has been done for you.

430 ÷ 5 = $\boxed{86}$

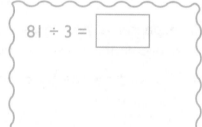

98 ÷ 7 = ☐

81 ÷ 3 = ☐

678 ÷ 6 = ☐

488 ÷ 8 = ☐

924 ÷ 4 = ☐

What you need to know   At this stage your child is learning to solve more complex multiplication and division problems using their known multiplication and division facts for **multiplication tables** up to **12 × 12**. They are learning how to multiply and divide **2-digit** and **3-digit numbers** by a **1-digit number** using a written method of **short multiplication** and **short division**.

Game: Remainders after dividing

You need: a 1–6 dice, six different coloured counters each.

- Take turns to the roll the dice.
- Find a division fact with a remainder that matches the number shown on the dice. Cover the division fact with a counter.
- The first player to place three counters in a horizontal row wins!

97 ÷ 8	41 ÷ 6	53 ÷ 7	94 ÷ 11	32 ÷ 5	15 ÷ 4
76 ÷ 6	50 ÷ 8	51 ÷ 9	65 ÷ 12	75 ÷ 9	28 ÷ 3

Jolly joke

Have you heard the tale of the fraction wall?

I can't tell you, you'd never get over it!

Target 496

The birds are holding number cards.

TIP: You can use each digit more than once!

- Use the digits 1, 2 and 4 to make a 3-digit number that when multiplied by 4 is equal to 496.

- Use the digits 9 and 2 to make a 3-digit number that when divided by 2 is equal to 496.

Taking it further Talk further with your child about remainders. Ask them to think about the 6, 7, 8 and 9 multiplication tables and ask what would be the greatest remainder for each multiplication table. Ask your child to show this practically using pasta shells.

Problem solving

Answer these one-step problems.

1. I think of a number and subtract 124. The answer is 567. What is my number?

2. I think of a number and add 271. The answer is 985. What is my number?

3. Ben has 27 marbles. His sister Sarah has four times as many. How many marbles has Sarah got?

4. Damien is building a wooden block house. He has built half the house and has used 123 blocks. How many wooden blocks will he use for the complete house?

5. How many egg boxes, each holding 6 eggs, can be filled by 96 eggs?

6. There are five small pepperoni pizzas to be shared equally between ten friends. How much pizza will each friend get?

Two-step problems

Answer these two-step problems.

1. I am thinking of a number. I take away three then double and I get eighteen. What is my number?

2. In its first year the shop 'Shiny Wheels' sold 269 bikes. It sold 543 bikes in its second year. After three years the shop has sold 1045 bikes. How many bikes did the shop sell in its third year?

3. A cinema has 48 rows of seats. Each row has 9 seats. 27 seats have already been pre-booked online.

   a) How many seats are left to sell?

   b) How many seats are left, to nearest 100?

What you need to know At this stage your child is learning to solve **one-step** and **two-step problems**, choosing the appropriate **operations** (i.e. **add**, **subtract**, **multiply**, **divide**).

Game: Sunday roast

You need: a pencil and paper each.

- Look at the menu. You can choose one roast meat and two vegetables.

- List all the different meals you can choose.

- Try to beat your opponent by finding more ways to make different meals than them.

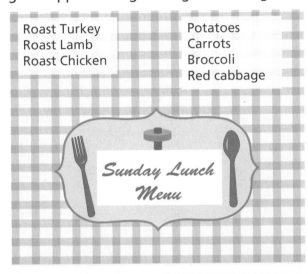

Roast Turkey
Roast Lamb
Roast Chicken

Potatoes
Carrots
Broccoli
Red cabbage

Sunday Lunch Menu

Jolly joke

Why was the maths book unhappy?

It had too many problems!

Monkey puzzle

Solve this monkey puzzle.

Charlie the monkey had between 10 and 30 bananas.

He counted the bananas in threes. There were two left over.

He counted the bananas in fives. There were three left over.

- How many bananas did Charlie have?

Taking it further Ask your child how they can check if their answers to the word problems on page 22 are sensible, without looking at the answers? Explain that they can use the inverse operations to check. They can also estimate the answers by rounding the numbers in each problem to the nearest 10 or 100 before completing the calculations. Ask your child to check their answers using either approach.

Fractions

- Fill in the missing hundredths.

$\frac{1}{100}$	$\frac{2}{100}$		$\frac{4}{100}$	$\frac{5}{100}$	$\frac{6}{100}$		$\frac{8}{100}$		$\frac{10}{100}$
$\frac{11}{100}$		$\frac{13}{100}$	$\frac{14}{100}$		$\frac{16}{100}$	$\frac{17}{100}$	$\frac{18}{100}$		$\frac{20}{100}$
	$\frac{22}{100}$	$\frac{23}{100}$		$\frac{25}{100}$	$\frac{26}{100}$		$\frac{28}{100}$	$\frac{29}{100}$	
$\frac{31}{100}$		$\frac{33}{100}$	$\frac{34}{100}$		$\frac{36}{100}$	$\frac{37}{100}$		$\frac{39}{100}$	
	$\frac{42}{100}$	$\frac{43}{100}$		$\frac{45}{100}$		$\frac{47}{100}$		$\frac{49}{100}$	$\frac{50}{100}$
$\frac{51}{100}$		$\frac{53}{100}$	$\frac{54}{100}$		$\frac{56}{100}$		$\frac{58}{100}$	$\frac{59}{100}$	
	$\frac{62}{100}$		$\frac{64}{100}$	$\frac{65}{100}$		$\frac{67}{100}$		$\frac{69}{100}$	
$\frac{71}{100}$		$\frac{73}{100}$		$\frac{75}{100}$		$\frac{77}{100}$	$\frac{78}{100}$		$\frac{80}{100}$
	$\frac{82}{100}$	$\frac{83}{100}$	$\frac{84}{100}$		$\frac{86}{100}$		$\frac{88}{100}$	$\frac{89}{100}$	
$\frac{91}{100}$	$\frac{92}{100}$		$\frac{94}{100}$	$\frac{95}{100}$		$\frac{97}{100}$		$\frac{99}{100}$	

Fraction decimal equivalents

- Draw a line to match each decimal to its equivalent fraction.

0.4　　**0.25**　　**0.6**　　**0.5**　　**0.75**　　**0.02**

$\frac{4}{10}$　　$\frac{3}{4}$　　$\frac{1}{4}$　　$\frac{2}{100}$　　$\frac{6}{10}$　　$\frac{1}{2}$

What you need to know　At this stage your child is learning to count up and down in **hundredths**. They should know that a hundredth is when one whole object is divided into a hundred equal parts and is the same as dividing a tenth into ten. They are learning to recognise **equivalent fractions** and also to write **decimal equivalents** for common fractions.

Examples are $\frac{1}{2} = 0.5$, $\frac{1}{4} = 0.25$, $\frac{3}{4} = 0.75$ and $\frac{1}{10} = 0.1$

Game: Fraction equivalents

You need: a paper clip, a different coloured pencil each.

- Take turns to spin the spinner. Find a fraction on the grid below that is equivalent to the fraction on the spinner. Colour the fraction.

- The first player to colour three fractions in a row (vertical, horizontal or diagonal) wins!

$\frac{5}{10}$	$\frac{2}{6}$	$\frac{2}{8}$	$\frac{8}{24}$	$\frac{6}{12}$
$\frac{12}{24}$	$\frac{4}{6}$	$\frac{4}{8}$	$\frac{18}{24}$	$\frac{3}{6}$
$\frac{3}{12}$	$\frac{6}{8}$	$\frac{6}{24}$	$\frac{4}{12}$	$\frac{8}{12}$

Spinner: $\frac{1}{2}$ $\frac{3}{4}$ $\frac{1}{3}$ $\frac{2}{3}$ $\frac{1}{4}$

TIP: You can use the fraction wall to help.

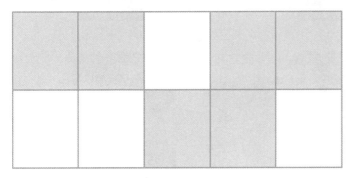

Fraction and decimal puzzle

Jolly joke

Who invented fractions?

Henry the $\frac{1}{8}$th

- How much of this shape is shaded?

  Give your answer as a fraction and a decimal.

Fraction

Decimal

Taking it further Look at the hundredths square (page 24) and practise counting up and down in hundredths. Select different hundredths values from the hundredths square; ask your child to write the decimal equivalents for each of these.

25

More fractions

- Fill in the boxes to show what the fraction is. Write the fraction where the arrow is pointing.

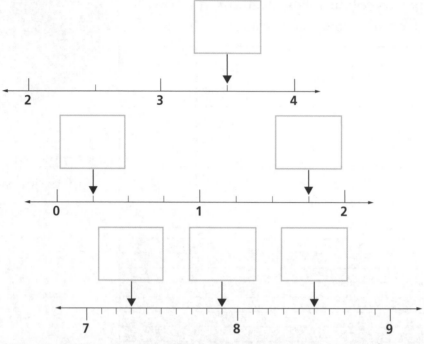

Fraction calculations

- Answer these fraction calculations.

$\frac{5}{4} + \frac{2}{4}$ = ☐

$\frac{7}{5} - \frac{3}{5}$ = ☐

$\frac{1}{5}$ of 45 = ☐

$\frac{3}{5} + \frac{1}{5}$ = ☐

$\frac{8}{9} - \frac{5}{9}$ = ☐

$\frac{6}{7}$ of 49 = ☐

$\frac{6}{8} + \frac{4}{8}$ = ☐

$\frac{10}{12} - \frac{4}{12}$ = ☐

$\frac{5}{9}$ of 108 = ☐

What you need to know At this stage your child is learning to count in **simple fractions**, both forwards and backwards. They are learning to **add** and **subtract fractions** with the **same denominator beyond one whole**, e.g. $\frac{5}{6} + \frac{4}{6} = \frac{9}{6}$. They will continue to practise **how to find fractions of amounts** using more challenging fractions, e.g. $\frac{4}{5}$ of an amount or $\frac{7}{9}$ of an amount.

Game: Adding sixths!

You need: a 1–6 dice, a pencil, paper.

- Take turns to roll the dice. The number rolled will be the numerator.

- As a dice has six faces, 6 will be the denominator for each fraction.

> **Example:** If you roll 5 your fraction will be $\frac{5}{6}$.

- Roll the dice again to make another fraction.

- Add both the fractions together and write your answer down.

- The player with the larger number of sixths scores a point.

- After five rounds, the player with more points wins!

> **TIP:** The 'numerator' is the number on the 'top' of a fraction. The 'denominator' is the number under the line.

Megan's prize money

Jolly joke

What can a whole orange do that half an orange cannot?
Look round!

Work out this problem.

> Megan won £600 from a radio competition.
>
> She spent $\frac{1}{3}$ of her winnings on a very smart watch.
>
> She spent $\frac{1}{6}$ of her winnings on the latest mobile phone.
>
> Finally, she spent $\frac{1}{4}$ of her winnings on a new plasma TV.

- How much money does she have left to save?

Taking it further   When you are out and about encourage your child to take notice of fractions and decimals in real life. An example would be in a supermarket, where you can see 'half price' items or a 'third off' selected items. Ask your child to use their knowledge of fractions to calculate the new price.

Area and perimeter

- Work out the perimeter of each vegetable garden.

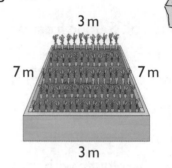

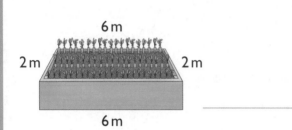

6 m

2 m   2 m

6 m

_____

3 m

7 m   7 m

3 m

_____

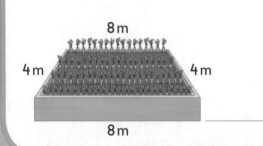

8 m

4 m   4 m

8 m

_____

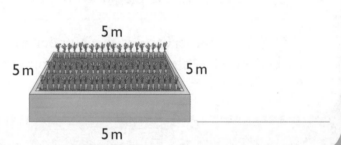

5 m

5 m   5 m

5 m

_____

Area

A farmer is measuring his fields.

- Count the squares to find the area of each field. Each square is equal to 1 m².

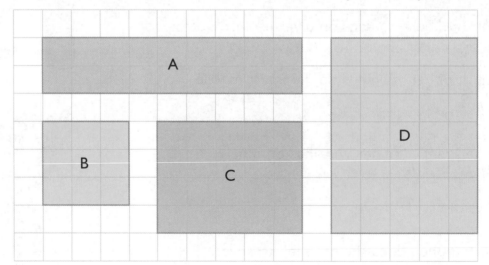

A = _____   B = _____   C = _____   D = _____

What you need to know   At this stage your child is learning to **measure** and calculate the **perimeter** of rectangular and square shapes in centimetres and metres by adding up the lengths around the total distance of the shape. They are also learning to find the **area** (the surface area the shape covers) by counting the number of squares.

Game: Smallest perimeter!

You need: a 1–6 dice, a ruler, a pencil, paper.

- Take turns to roll the dice twice.

- Draw a rectangle accurately, using a ruler and the two numbers you rolled.

  Example: If you roll 6 and 4 you can draw this rectangle:

  6 cm

  4 cm   4 cm

  6 cm

- Find the perimeter of your rectangle.

- The player with the rectangle with the smaller perimeter wins a point.

- Play five rounds. The player with more points wins!

Jolly joke

Where are teachers made?

On an assembly line!

Garden lawn puzzle

A gardener wants a rectangular lawn with an area of 12 m².

- On the grid, draw as many gardens as possible that have an area of 12 m².
  Each square is equal to 1 m².

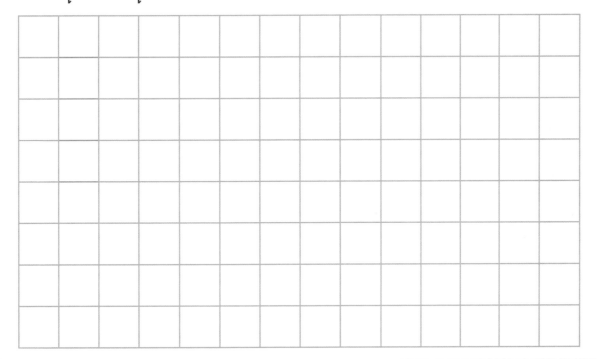

Taking it further Ask your child to consider whether the perimeter will be the same for all of the different lawns with an area of 12 m². Ask them to prove their thinking by calculating the perimeter of each lawn. Watch how your child calculates the perimeter. Are they adding each length and width up individually, e.g. for a lawn measuring 3 m × 4 m, do they calculate the perimeter by adding 3 m + 3 m + 4 m + 4 m? If they do, ask how they could be more efficient. Encourage your child to use the formula 2 × (3 m + 4 m).

Measures

- Fill in the missing lengths.

I cm = [ ] mm   12 cm = [ ] mm   5.5 cm = [ ] mm

I m = [ ] cm   5 m = [ ] cm $7\frac{1}{4}$ m = [ ] cm

I km = [ ] m   2 km = [ ] m $2\frac{1}{2}$ km = [ ] m

Ordering scales

- Put these scales in order, from the heaviest to the lightest.

A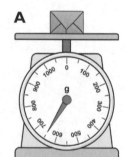

B

C

D

E

F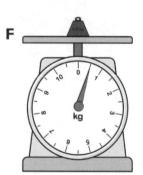

Heaviest [ ] [ ] [ ] [ ] [ ] [ ] Lightest

Game: Measures loop

Jolly joke

Why did the boy put a ruler on his bed?

To measure how long he slept!

You need: a knowledge of key facts about measures.

- Player 1 begins with asking the 'red' question on the start card.

- Player 2 finds the card with the answer and then reads the 'red' question on that card.

- Player 1 then looks for the card with the answer. The player then reads the question on that card.

- Keep taking turns until you reach the end card.

START	I have 150 cm	I have 14 cm	I have 1700 g	I have 1.2 kg
Who has 1 cm in mm?	Who has 140 mm in cm?	Who has 4.3 kg in g?	Who has $1\frac{1}{2}$ m in cm?	Who has 1000 ml in litres?

I have 1 litre	I have 4.8 cm	I have 2500 ml	I have 10 mm	I have 0.2 kg
Who has 1.7 kg in g?	Who has 1200 g in kg?	Who has 200 g in kg?	Who has 2 kg in g?	Who has $1\frac{3}{4}$ m in cm?

I have 2000 g	I have 4300 g	I have 700 cm	I have 175 cm	I have 0.3 litres
Who has 300 ml in litres?	Who has 2.5 litres in ml?	Who has 48 mm in cm?	**END CARD**	Who has 7 m in cm?

Measures

Solve this measure problem.

> Dad needs 15 litres of water to wash his car. He decides to fill a bucket using a 2500 ml jug and a 250 ml cup.

2500 ml

15 litres

250 ml

- Write three different ways he can fill the bucket using the jug and/or the cup.

Taking it further Encourage your child to use scales at home by asking to them to help measure the ingredients for a simple recipe. Also, give them practical experiences of comparing how much liquid different containers hold. For example, will a short and wide jug hold more than or less than a tall and narrow container?

Money

This is a menu at a cafe.

Cold sandwiches		Drinks	
All served with salad.		Mug of tea	£0.70
Ham	£2.55	Pot of tea	£1.60
Cheese	£1.95	Coffee	£1.10
Tuna	£2.10	Juice	£0.95
Chicken mayonnaise	£2.35		
Egg and cress	£1.80		
Turkey	£2.15		

● How much money did each person spend at the cafe?

 Amir — Tuna sandwich + Mug of tea

 Kate — Chicken mayonnaise sandwich + Coffee

 Matt — Turkey sandwich + Pot of tea

 Reena — Egg and cress sandwich + Ham sandwich + 2 juices

● How much change would each person get if they paid for their food bill using a £10 note?

Game: Holiday spending

You need: a 1–6 dice, a pencil each, paper.

Mrs Ling went on holiday to Canada for one week.
How much did the holiday cost altogether?

- Take turns to roll the dice. Match the number rolled to the clue card number below.

- If the information is helpful for you to solve the problem then write it down.

- Once you have collected all the key information from the clue cards, solve the problem.

- The player to solve the problem first wins!

Clue 1
The hotel cost £63 per night.

Clue 2
The return flight cost £1075.

Clue 3
Mrs Ling visited Niagra Falls.

Clue 4
She spent £95.50 of her spending money.

Clue 5
The weather was very hot!

Clue 6
Taxi costs were £41.64.

Jolly joke

Where do fish keep their money?

In the River Bank!

Presents

Sam paid £15 for three presents.

- 🎁 For A and B he paid a total of £8.
- 🎁 For B and C he paid a total of £12.
- 🎁 For A and C he paid a total of £10.

- How much did Sam pay for each present?

A: _____   B: _____   C: _____

Time

12-hour and 24-hour clocks

- Draw lines to match the 12-hour and 24-hour times on these digital clocks.

| 7:30 P.M. | 8:15 A.M. | 8:15 P.M. | 2:54 A.M. | 2:54 P.M. |

| 08:15 | 14:54 | 02:54 | 20:15 | 19:30 |

Writing 24-hour times

- Write the 24-hour times on these digital clock faces.

Twenty past three in the afternoon

| : |

Ten past six in the morning

| : |

Quarter past ten in the evening

| : |

Ten to four in the afternoon

| : |

2 minutes past one in the morning

| : |

20 minutes to three in the afternoon

| : |

09:00

10:00

What you need to know   At this stage your child is learning to **convert time** between a **12-hour clock** and a **24-hour clock**. They are learning to **solve time problems**, involving converting from **hours** to **minutes**, minutes to **seconds**, **years** to **months**, **weeks** to **days** and vice versa.

Game: Time differences

You need: a paper clip, a set of different coloured counters each, a pencil.

- Take turns to spin the spinner. Look at the grid and find two times (one of each colour) with a time difference to match the time on the spinner. Cover both the times with counters.

- If you cannot find two times with a time difference shown on the spinner, miss your turn.

- The player with the most counters after five rounds wins!

2 hours 10 minutes	30 minutes
45 minutes	1 hour 15 minutes

16:00	12:36	09:30	10:17
12:15	19:50	09:00	22:15
17:06	05:49	12:06	19:16
07:59	22:45	12:27	08:45
15:45	11:30	10:30	20:20
17:00	18:35	17:50	17:15

Jolly joke

Why did the student throw his watch out of the window?

To see time fly!

Time fact quiz

Answer these questions.

1. It takes Susan 100 minutes to cycle to work. How long is that in hours and minutes?

2. Jay and his family went on holiday for 16 days. How many weeks and days were they away?

3. It took an athlete 275 seconds to run a 1500 metre race. How long was that in minutes and seconds?

4. Jack will be celebrating his 10th birthday in 16 months. How many years and months away is this?

Taking it further Give your child lots of practice with converting between 12-hour and 24-hour clocks. Build it into your daily routine, e.g. we are going to eat dinner at quarter past 7 this evening, what time is this using the 24-hour clock?

More problem solving

1. Priya buys one watermelon and half a kilogram of grapes. How much does she spend altogether?

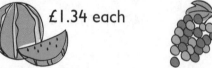 £1.34 each 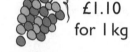 £1.10 for 1 kg

2. One length of the swimming pool is 25 metres.
   a) Tom swims nine lengths of the pool. How far does he swim altogether?

   b) Alice swims 200 metres. How many lengths does she swim?

3.

Equipment to hire on the slopes	
Snowboard: £2.50 for 30 minutes	Skis: £1.20 for 1 hour 15 minutes

   a) How much does it cost to hire a snowboard for 1 hour?

   b) How much does it cost to hire skis for 2 hours 30 minutes?

Roman numeral puzzle

- Using these Roman numerals:

   I = 1   V = 5   X = 10   L = 50   C = 100

   convert the numbers shown below into Roman numerals.

   6 =   15 =   21 =   40 =

   50 =   70 =   85 =   95 =

What you need to know   At this stage your child is learning to **solve money** and **measure problems** involving **one-step** and **two-step problems**. They are expected to **choose** the appropriate operations (i.e. **add**, **subtract**, **multiply**, **divide**) and convert between **different units** of measure to solve the problems. They are also learning to read Roman numerals to 100 (I to C).

Game: Making word problems

You need: two paper clips, two pencils, paper.

- Spin the two spinners to find which operation to use and what your problem needs to be about. If you are making up a two-step problem then you'll have to spin the 'operation spinner' twice.

- Take turns to make up and write word problems, each time solving the problem together.

TIP: Look at the mixed word problems on page 36 for examples of the type of problems you should make up.

capacity l, ml	money £, p
weight kg, g	length m, cm

÷	+
×	−

Jolly joke

What makes maths hard work?

All those numbers you have to carry!

Bear club sandwiches

Here are the ingredients needed to make 1 bear club sandwich.

10 g of butter   1 slice of ham   3 slices of cheese
2 slices of bread   2 slices of tomato   4 salad leaves

- Write the ingredients needed to make sandwiches for the three bears.

$\frac{1}{2}$ a sandwich for baby bear's lunch box

6 sandwiches for daddy bear's long drive

9 sandwiches for mummy bear's tea party

Taking it further   Ask your child how they can check how sensible their answers are to the word problems on page 36 – without looking at the answer pages. Explain that they can use the inverse operations to check but that they can also estimate the answer by rounding the numbers in the problem to the nearest 10 or 100 before completing the calculation. Ask your child to check their answers using both approaches.

Angles

- Write the number of each quadrilateral under the correct heading in the table.

No right angles	I right angle	2 or more right angles

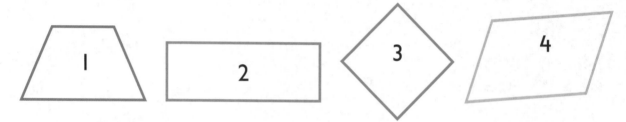

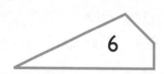
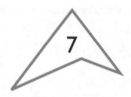

Ordering angles

- Order the angles from smallest to largest.

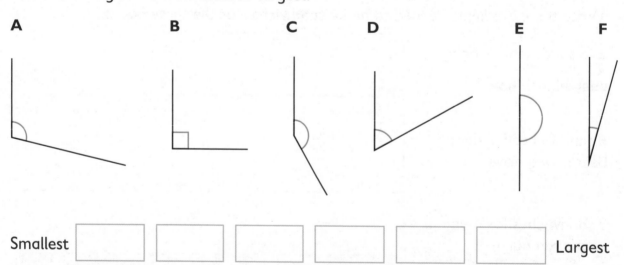

A   B   C   D   E   F

Smallest | | | | | | | | | | | Largest

What you need to know   At this stage your child is learning to identify **acute angles** (less than 90°) and **obtuse angles** (more than 90° but less than 180°). They are also learning to **order a range of angles by size** up to two **right angles** (i.e. 180°).

Game: Acute or obtuse

You need: a 1–6 dice, a different coloured pencil each.

- Take turns to roll the dice. If the number is even, colour that number of acute angles. If it is odd, colour that number of obtuse angles.

> **Example:** If you roll 2, colour two acute angles.
> If you roll 5, colour five obtuse angles.

- If there are not enough of the angles you need to colour, miss a turn.
- Stop when all the angles are coloured.
- The winner is the player who has coloured more angles.

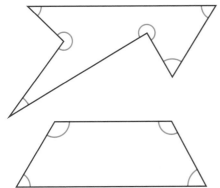
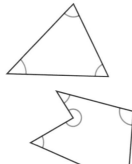
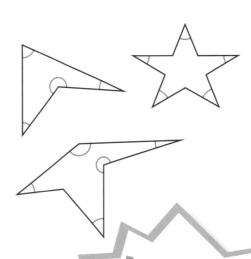

Jolly joke

What do you call a pretty angle that is adorable?

Acute angle!

Angles on the clock

- Draw an hour hand on each clock face to show these angles:

1. An acute angle

2. A right angle

3. An obtuse angle

Taking it further Look at a clock face with your child at various times during the day. Work out if the angle on the clock face is acute or obtuse.

Quadrilaterals and triangles

Triangles

- Write a letter on each triangle below: I = isosceles E = equilateral S = scalene

Properties of quadrilaterals

- Label each shape with its name.
- Now draw a line to match each shape to its properties box.

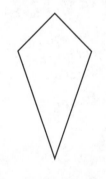

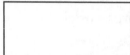

• 2 pairs of equal sides next to each other • No parallel sides.
• 2 pairs of equal sides • Opposite sides are parallel • Opposite angles are equal • No right angles
• 2 pairs of equal sides • 4 right angles
• 4 equal sides • 4 right angles
• One pair of parallel sides of different lengths
• 4 equal sides • Opposite sides are parallel • Opposite angles are equal and are not right angles

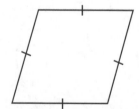

What you need to know At this stage your child is learning to identify the properties of these shapes:
- **Quadrilaterals** (four-sided shapes): square, rectangle, parallelogram, trapezium, rhombus, kite.
- **Triangles**: right-angled, isosceles, scalene, equilateral.

Game: Guess my triangle

You need: a pencil each, paper.

- Player 1 chooses a triangle from page 40 and writes down the name of the triangle chosen. Do not show this to your opponent.

- Player 2 asks two key questions about the triangle's properties. Player 1 answers the questions, using "yes" or "no".

- Player 2 tries to work out the type of triangle from the answers given and checks to see if it matches the triangle that player 1 chose. If it does, then player 2 scores a point.

- Swap roles each time. After three goes each, the player with more points wins!

Jolly joke

What triangles are coldest?

Ice-sosceles triangles!

Quadrilaterals

A quadrilateral has been drawn below.

- Draw five more different quadrilaterals by joining up the dots with a ruler.

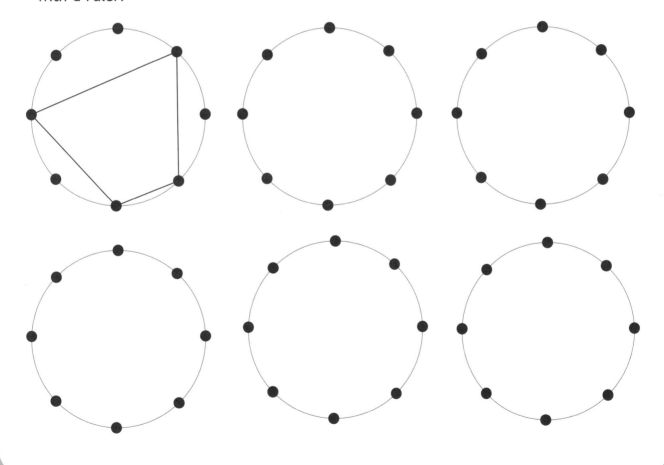

Taking it further Ask your child to look for different triangles and quadrilaterals around the home. Can they give the correct name of the shape and identify the properties of that particular shape?

Symmetry

- Draw a line of symmetry on each shape.

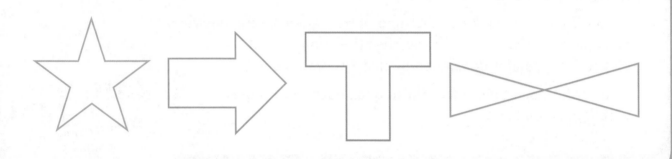

Symmetrical patterns

- Complete these symmetrical patterns.

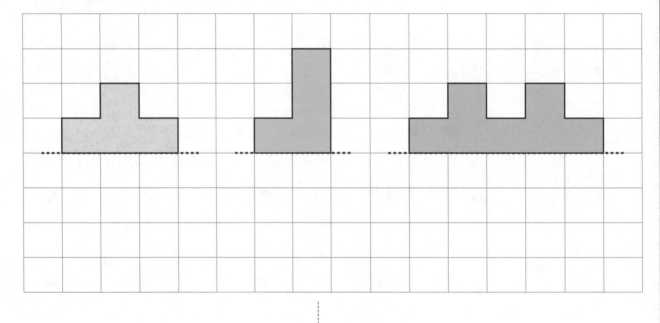

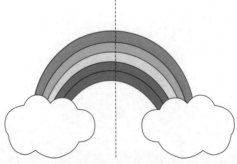

What you need to know   At this stage your child is learning to recognise **lines of symmetry** in a range of shapes and diagrams. They are also learning to draw **symmetrical patterns**.

Game: Symmetrical lines

You need: a 1–6 dice, a different coloured counter each, a pencil, paper.

- Place the counters on **start**.

- Take turns to roll the dice.

- Move your counter along the shape board according to the number on the dice.

Score card	
Lines of symmetry	Points
1 line	4
2 lines	6
3 lines	8
4 lines	10
5 lines	12

- Look at the shape you land on and find the total number of lines of symmetry. Use the score card and award yourself the correct amount of points.

- Keep a running total of your points.

- Once both players have got to the end of the shape board the player who has more points wins!

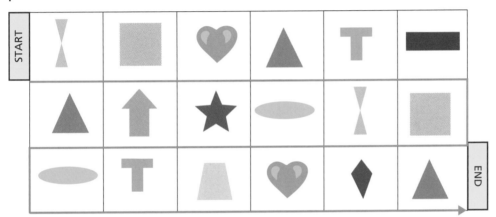

Symmetry investigation

- Draw the lines of symmetry on each of these regular polygons.

- What pattern do you notice? _____

Taking it further Ask your child to test further their findings from the symmetry investigation. Does their generalisation work for a regular octagon? Ask them how else they may prove what they have found so that they can be sure it works consistently for all regular polygons.

Coordinates

This grid shows the positions of four cars.

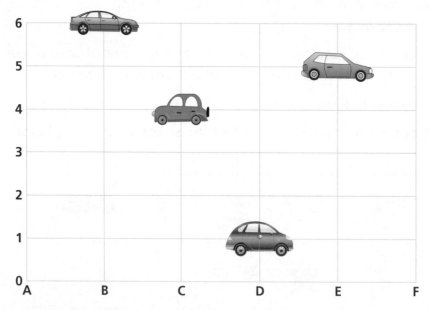

- Use coordinates to write the position of each car.

- On the grid, draw a car at (F, 3).

Translations

This grid shows the position of X.

- Move X right 2 and down 1. Write 'Y' in the new position on the grid.
- Now move X up 1 and left 1. Write 'Z' in the new position on the grid.

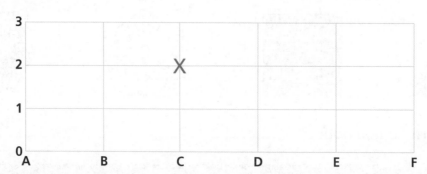

What you need to know   At this stage your child is learning to read, write and describe position on a 2D grid using **coordinates**, e.g. (C, 2). They are also describing movements between positions (up/down; left/right) as **translations**.

Game: Shape vertices

You need: a paper clip, a set of different coloured counters each, a pencil.

- Take turns to spin the spinner. Place a counter on the shape vertex that matches the coordinate on the spinner.
- Continue playing until all the vertices have been covered.
- If the vertex you spin already has a counter on it, miss a turn.
- If a player has managed to place a counter on all the vertices of at least one shape then they win.

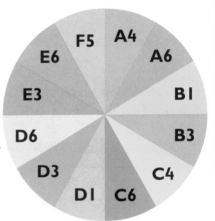

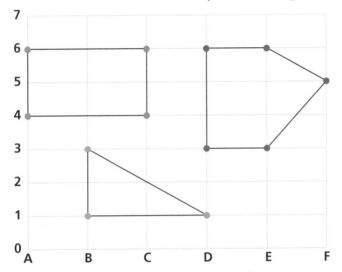

Jolly joke

How do you start a flea race?

Flea-two-one-GO!

Missing coordinate puzzle

The graph shows the coordinates of three shapes.

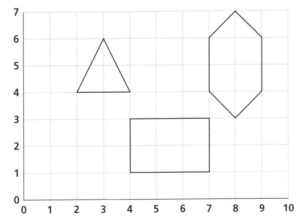

- Fill in the missing coordinates.

Triangle (2, ☐), (☐, 6), (4, 4)   Rectangle (4, ☐), (☐, 3), (☐, ☐), (7, 3)

Hexagon (7, 4), (☐, 3), (☐, 4), (9, ☐), (☐, 7), (☐, 6)

Taking it further Look at the positions of the cars again on page 44. Ask your child to give you directions to park the cars at different positions on the grid. Encourage them to use the correct positional language, e.g. up, left, right, down.

Graphs

Some children were asked about their favourite sports. The bar chart shows the results.

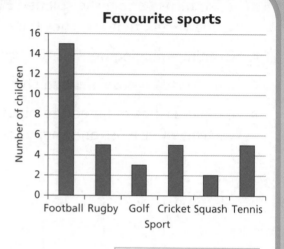

Favourite sports

- Which is the most popular sport?

- How many children prefer cricket?

- In total, how many children said rugby, cricket or tennis is their favourite?

- How many more children like golf than squash?

- How many more children prefer football to rugby?

- What is the difference between the number of children who chose cricket and the number who chose football?

Time graph

The time graph shows how long it takes to fill a bath.

Bath time

- What was the water level after 1 minute?

- What was the water level after 2 minutes?

- What was the water level after 3 minutes?

- How many minutes did it take to fill the bath to 35 cm?

What you need to know At this stage your child is learning to interpret **discrete data** and **continuous data**. They will answer questions about data in the form of **bar charts**, **time graphs**, **pictograms**, **tables** and other graphs.

Note: discrete data has individual separate data points that cannot be split up, e.g. favourite colours, while continuous data will have an infinite number of possible values on a scale, e.g. heights of students in a class.

Game: Pictogram

You need: a coin, a set of different coloured counters each.

● Take turns to toss a coin.

● If you toss 'Heads' then use a counter to cover a statement about the pictogram that is **true**. If you toss 'Tails' then use a counter to cover a statement about the pictogram that is **false**. If you cannot cover a statement, miss a turn.

● When all statements have been covered, the player who covered more statements wins!

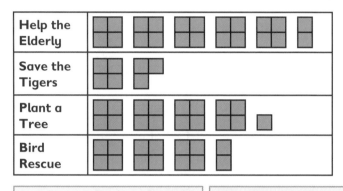

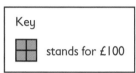

Help the Elderly has raised £550.	*Bird Rescue* has raised £50 more than *Save the Tigers*.	*Save the Tigers* has raised £1$\frac{3}{4}$.
Save the Tigers has made £200 rounded to the nearest hundred.	*Plant a Tree* needs to raise another £175 to make £500.	*Bird Rescue* has raised £75 more than *Save the Tigers*.
Help the Elderly and *Plant a Tree* have raised over £1000 together.	*Plant a Tree* has raised £4.25.	*Save the Tigers* and *Bird Rescue* have raised £425 together.
Bird Rescue needs to raise another £50 to make £300.	*Save the Tigers* has raised £175.	*Bird Rescue* is halfway to making its target of £500.

Rainfall

● Use the Internet to find the total monthly rainfall over a period of six months for a town near you.

● Plot these on the bar chart below.

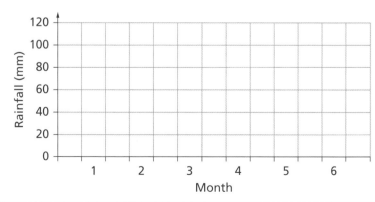

Jolly joke

Is your statistics joke any good?

No, it's just average – but I feel mean telling you!

Taking it further Ask your child to carry out a survey of their choice looking at either discrete or continuous data. Ask your child to use this information to form a table and then draw either a bar chart or graph, depending on the data chosen.

Answers

Pages 4–5

Place value
300, 30, 3, 3000
9000, 900, 9, 90

Comparing and ordering
1172, 1112, 1023, 1010
9876 m, 9754 m, 8692 m, 8541 m
7957 kg, 7257 kg, 6010 kg, 5334 kg

Missing numbers
3753 = 3000 + 700 + 50 + 3
5967 = 5000 + 900 + 60 + 7
4639 = 4000 + 600 + 30 + 9
1398 = 1000 + 300 + 90 + 8

Pages 6–7

1000 more
3315, 8892, 1786, 1912

1000 less
7476, 4892, 1934, 279

True or false
True; True; False

Pages 8–9

Rounding 3-digit numbers to the nearest 10 and 100
190 km, 200 km   190 km, 200 km
310 km, 300 km   130 km, 100 km

Rounding 4-digit numbers to the nearest 10, 100 and 1000
£1670, £1700, £2000
£5240, £5200, £5000

Rounding possibilities
975, 976, 977, 978, 979, 980, 981, 982, 983, 984
695, 696, 697, 698, 699, 700, 701, 702, 703, 704

Pages 10–11

Number sequences
6, 12, 18, 24, 30, 36, 42, 48, 54, 60, 66
7, 14, 21, 28, 35, 42, 49, 56, 63, 70, 77
9, 18, 27, 36, 45, 54, 63, 72, 81, 90, 99

Negative numbers
10, 9, 8, 7, 6, 5, 4, 3, 2, 1, 0, –1, –2, –3, –4, –5, –6, –7, –8, –9, –10
50, 45, 40, 35, 30, 25, 20, 15, 10, 5, 0, –5, – 10, –15, –20, –25, –30, –35, –40, –45, –50

Dice magic
The opposite two sides of a dice always add up to 7. With two dice = 7 × 2, so total will always be 14.

Pages 12–13

Place value
$\frac{7}{10}, \frac{7}{100}, 7, 7, \frac{7}{100}$

Comparing and ordering
3.70 kg, 3.22 kg, 3.12 kg, 2.86 kg
£2.81, £2.79, £2.56, £2.01
4.95ℓ, 4.85ℓ, 4.84ℓ, 3.25ℓ

Within limits
Possible answers are decimal numbers between 5.01 and 5.49.

Pages 14–15

Adding large whole numbers
4806, 6999
3788, 7920, 16825

Subtracting large whole numbers
4061, 2213
1105, 706, 3871

Missing digits
☆ = 7   ★ = 2   ☆ = 8
☆ = 4   ★ = 9

Pages 16–17

Multiplication grid

×	1	2	3	4	5	6	7	8	9	10	11	12
2	2	4	6	8	10	12	14	16	18	20	22	24
3	3	6	9	12	15	18	21	24	27	30	33	36
4	4	8	12	16	20	24	28	32	36	40	44	48
5	5	10	15	20	25	30	35	40	45	50	55	60
6	6	12	18	24	30	36	42	48	54	60	66	72
7	7	14	21	28	35	42	49	56	63	70	77	84
8	8	16	24	32	40	48	56	64	72	80	88	96
9	9	18	27	36	45	54	63	72	81	90	99	108
10	10	20	30	40	50	60	70	80	90	100	110	120
11	11	22	33	44	55	66	77	88	99	110	121	132
12	12	24	36	48	60	72	84	96	108	120	132	144

Division detective
Check your child's division facts are correct.

Herb pot factor pairs
6 × 2
1 × 24, 2 × 12, 4 × 6
1 × 18, 2 × 9, 3 × 6

Pages 18–19

Multiplying by 10 and 100
40, 90, 170, 350, 780
600, 200, 2100, 3800, 9500

Dividing by 10 and 100
0.5, 0.8, 0.9, 4.1, 5.2
0.01, 0.03, 0.07, 0.64, 0.88

Toy boxes
Height = 0.52 m, Length = 76 cm

Pages 20–21

Multiplying larger numbers
476, 1884, 3689, 1480, 2511

Dividing larger numbers
14, 27, 113, 61, 231

Target 496
124
992

Pages 22–23

One-step problems
1. 691 **2.** 714 **3.** 108 marbles
4. 246 blocks **5.** 16 egg boxes
6. half a pizza or 0.5

Two-step problems
1. 12 **2.** 233 bikes
3. a) 405 seats **b)** 400 seats

Monkey puzzle
23 bananas

Pages 24–25

Counting in hundredths

1/100	2/100	3/100	4/100	5/100	6/100	7/100	8/100	9/100	10/100
11/100	12/100	13/100	14/100	15/100	16/100	17/100	18/100	19/100	20/100
21/100	22/100	23/100	24/100	25/100	26/100	27/100	28/100	29/100	30/100
31/100	32/100	33/100	34/100	35/100	36/100	37/100	38/100	39/100	40/100
41/100	42/100	43/100	44/100	45/100	46/100	47/100	48/100	49/100	50/100
51/100	52/100	53/100	54/100	55/100	56/100	57/100	58/100	59/100	60/100
61/100	62/100	63/100	64/100	65/100	66/100	67/100	68/100	69/100	70/100
71/100	72/100	73/100	74/100	75/100	76/100	77/100	78/100	79/100	80/100
81/100	82/100	83/100	84/100	85/100	86/100	87/100	88/100	89/100	90/100
91/100	92/100	93/100	94/100	95/100	96/100	97/100	98/100	99/100	100/100

Fraction decimal equivalents

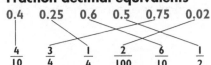

0.4   0.25   0.6   0.5   0.75   0.02

$\frac{4}{10}$ $\frac{3}{4}$ $\frac{1}{4}$ $\frac{2}{100}$ $\frac{6}{10}$ $\frac{1}{2}$

Fraction and decimal puzzle
$\frac{6}{10}$, 0.6

Pages 26–27

Counting in fractions
$3\frac{1}{2}; \frac{1}{4}, 1\frac{3}{4}; 7\frac{3}{10}, 7\frac{9}{10}, 8\frac{1}{2}$

Fraction calculations
$\frac{7}{4} (=1\frac{3}{4}), \frac{4}{5}, 9$

$\frac{4}{5}, \frac{3}{9} (=\frac{1}{3}), 42$

$\frac{10}{8} (=1\frac{2}{8} = 1\frac{1}{4}), \frac{6}{12} (=\frac{1}{2}), 60$